# Walk By Faith

*"Today, I've decided to close my eyes and trust that my Father is walking with me."*

# Walk By Faith

*"Today, I've decided to close my eyes and trust that
my Father is walking with me."*

# Walk By Faith

_"Today, I've decided to close my eyes and trust that_
_my Father is walking with me."_

# Walk By Faith

*"Today, I've decided to close my eyes and trust that my Father is walking with me."*

# Walk By Faith

*"Today, I've decided to close my eyes and trust that
my Father is walking with me."*

# Walk By Faith

# Walk By Faith

*"Today, I've decided to close my eyes and trust that my Father is walking with me."*

# Walk By Faith

"*Today, I've decided to close my eyes and trust that my Father is walking with me.*"

# Walk By Faith

*"Today, I've decided to close my eyes and trust that my Father is walking with me."*

# Walk By Faith

*"Today, I've decided to close my eyes and trust that
my Father is walking with me."*

# Walk By Faith

_"Today, I've decided to close my eyes and trust that
my Father is walking with me."_

# Walk By Faith

*"Today, I've decided to close my eyes and trust that
my Father is walking with me."*

# Walk By Faith

*"Today, I've decided to close my eyes and trust that my Father is walking with me."*

# Walk By Faith

_"Today, I've decided to close my eyes and trust that
my Father is walking with me."_

# Walk By Faith

_"Today, I've decided to close my eyes and trust that
my Father is walking with me."_

# Walk By Faith

# Walk By Faith

*"Today, I've decided to close my eyes and trust that
my Father is walking with me."*

# Walk By Faith

# Walk By Faith

*"Today, I've decided to close my eyes and trust that my Father is walking with me."*

# Walk By Faith

*"Today, I've decided to close my eyes and trust that my Father is walking with me."*

# Walk By Faith

_"Today, I've decided to close my eyes and trust that my Father is walking with me."_

# Walk By Faith

*"Today, I've decided to close my eyes and trust that
my Father is walking with me."*

# Walk By Faith

# Walk By Faith

*"Today, I've decided to close my eyes and trust that
my Father is walking with me."*

# Walk By Faith

_"Today, I've decided to close my eyes and trust that
my Father is walking with me."_

# Walk By Faith

*"Today, I've decided to close my eyes and trust that
my Father is walking with me."*

# Walk By Faith

_____
_____
_____
_____
_____
_____
_____
_____
_____
_____
_____
_____
_____
_____
_____
_____
_____
_____

*"Today, I've decided to close my eyes and trust that
my Father is walking with me."*

# Walk By Faith

*"Today, I've decided to close my eyes and trust that
my Father is walking with me."*

# Walk By Faith

*"Today, I've decided to close my eyes and trust that my Father is walking with me."*

# Walk By Faith

*"Today, I've decided to close my eyes and trust that
my Father is walking with me."*

# Walk By Faith

_"Today, I've decided to close my eyes and trust that
my Father is walking with me."_

# Walk By Faith

*"Today, I've decided to close my eyes and trust that*
*my Father is walking with me."*

# Walk By Faith

*"Today, I've decided to close my eyes and trust that my Father is walking with me."*

# Walk By Faith

*"Today, I've decided to close my eyes and trust that
my Father is walking with me."*

# Walk By Faith

*"Today, I've decided to close my eyes and trust that my Father is walking with me."*

# Walk By Faith

*"Today, I've decided to close my eyes and trust that
my Father is walking with me."*

# Walk By Faith

*"Today, I've decided to close my eyes and trust that
my Father is walking with me."*

# Walk By Faith

*"Today, I've decided to close my eyes and trust that
my Father is walking with me."*

# Walk By Faith

*"Today, I've decided to close my eyes and trust that
my Father is walking with me."*

# Walk By Faith

_"Today, I've decided to close my eyes and trust that
my Father is walking with me."_

# Walk By Faith

*"Today, I've decided to close my eyes and trust that my Father is walking with me."*

# Walk By Faith

*"Today, I've decided to close my eyes and trust that my Father is walking with me."*

# Walk By Faith

_____
_____
_____
_____
_____
_____
_____
_____
_____
_____
_____
_____
_____
_____
_____
_____
_____
_____
_____
_____
_____
_____

*"Today, I've decided to close my eyes and trust that
my Father is walking with me."*

# Walk By Faith

*"Today, I've decided to close my eyes and trust that my Father is walking with me."*

# Walk By Faith

*"Today, I've decided to close my eyes and trust that my Father is walking with me."*

# Walk By Faith

*"Today, I've decided to close my eyes and trust that
my Father is walking with me."*

# Walk By Faith

*"Today, I've decided to close my eyes and trust that my Father is walking with me."*

# Walk By Faith

*"Today, I've decided to close my eyes and trust that my Father is walking with me."*

# Walk By Faith

*"Today, I've decided to close my eyes and trust that my Father is walking with me."*

# Walk By Faith

*"Today, I've decided to close my eyes and trust that my Father is walking with me."*

# Walk By Faith

*"Today, I've decided to close my eyes and trust that
my Father is walking with me."*

# Walk By Faith

*"Today, I've decided to close my eyes and trust that*
*my Father is walking with me."*

# Walk By Faith

# Walk By Faith

*"Today, I've decided to close my eyes and trust that*
*my Father is walking with me."*

# Walk By Faith

*"Today, I've decided to close my eyes and trust that my Father is walking with me."*

# Walk By Faith

*"Today, I've decided to close my eyes and trust that
my Father is walking with me."*

# Walk By Faith

*"Today, I've decided to close my eyes and trust that my Father is walking with me."*

# Walk By Faith

_"Today, I've decided to close my eyes and trust that
my Father is walking with me."_

# Walk By Faith

*"Today, I've decided to close my eyes and trust that my Father is walking with me."*

# Walk By Faith

*"Today, I've decided to close my eyes and trust that
my Father is walking with me."*

# Walk By Faith

_"Today, I've decided to close my eyes and trust that
my Father is walking with me."_

# Walk By Faith

*"Today, I've decided to close my eyes and trust that my Father is walking with me."*

# Walk By Faith

---

*"Today, I've decided to close my eyes and trust that my Father is walking with me."*

# Walk By Faith

*"Today, I've decided to close my eyes and trust that
my Father is walking with me."*

# Walk By Faith

*"Today, I've decided to close my eyes and trust that my Father is walking with me."*

# Walk By Faith

*"Today, I've decided to close my eyes and trust that
my Father is walking with me."*

# Walk By Faith

# Walk By Faith

*"Today, I've decided to close my eyes and trust that
my Father is walking with me."*

# Walk By Faith

_____

_____

_____

_____

_____

_____

_____

_____

_____

_____

_____

_____

_____

_____

_____

_____

_____

_____

_____

*"Today, I've decided to close my eyes and trust that
my Father is walking with me."*

# Walk By Faith

*"Today, I've decided to close my eyes and trust that
my Father is walking with me."*

# Walk By Faith

*"Today, I've decided to close my eyes and trust that
my Father is walking with me."*

# Walk By Faith

*"Today, I've decided to close my eyes and trust that
my Father is walking with me."*

# Walk By Faith

*"Today, I've decided to close my eyes and trust that my Father is walking with me."*

# Walk By Faith

_"Today, I've decided to close my eyes and trust that
my Father is walking with me."_

# Walk By Faith

*"Today, I've decided to close my eyes and trust that
my Father is walking with me."*

# Walk By Faith

*"Today, I've decided to close my eyes and trust that my Father is walking with me."*

# Walk By Faith

*"Today, I've decided to close my eyes and trust that
my Father is walking with me."*

# Walk By Faith

*"Today, I've decided to close my eyes and trust that
my Father is walking with me."*

# Walk By Faith

_"Today, I've decided to close my eyes and trust that
my Father is walking with me."_

# Walk By Faith

*"Today, I've decided to close my eyes and trust that my Father is walking with me."*

# Walk By Faith

_"Today, I've decided to close my eyes and trust that_
_my Father is walking with me."_

# Walk By Faith

*"Today, I've decided to close my eyes and trust that my Father is walking with me."*

# Walk By Faith

*"Today, I've decided to close my eyes and trust that
my Father is walking with me."*

# Walk By Faith

*"Today, I've decided to close my eyes and trust that
my Father is walking with me."*

# Walk By Faith

*"Today, I've decided to close my eyes and trust that
my Father is walking with me."*

# Walk By Faith

*"Today, I've decided to close my eyes and trust that
my Father is walking with me."*

# Walk By Faith

_"Today, I've decided to close my eyes and trust that
my Father is walking with me."_

# Walk By Faith

*"Today, I've decided to close my eyes and trust that*
*my Father is walking with me."*

# Walk By Faith

*"Today, I've decided to close my eyes and trust that
my Father is walking with me."*

# Walk By Faith

*"Today, I've decided to close my eyes and trust that
my Father is walking with me."*

# Walk By Faith

_____

_____

_____

_____

_____

_____

_____

_____

_____

_____

_____

_____

_____

_____

_____

_____

_____

_____

_____

*"Today, I've decided to close my eyes and trust that
my Father is walking with me."*

# Walk By Faith

_"Today, I've decided to close my eyes and trust that
my Father is walking with me."_

# Walk By Faith

_"Today, I've decided to close my eyes and trust that
my Father is walking with me."_

# Walk By Faith

*"Today, I've decided to close my eyes and trust that my Father is walking with me."*

# Walk By Faith

_"Today, I've decided to close my eyes and trust that
my Father is walking with me."_

# Walk By Faith

*"Today, I've decided to close my eyes and trust that*
*my Father is walking with me."*

# Walk By Faith

_"Today, I've decided to close my eyes and trust that
my Father is walking with me."_

# Walk By Faith

*"Today, I've decided to close my eyes and trust that my Father is walking with me."*

# Walk By Faith

*"Today, I've decided to close my eyes and trust that my Father is walking with me."*

# Walk By Faith

*"Today, I've decided to close my eyes and trust that
my Father is walking with me."*

# Walk By Faith

*"Today, I've decided to close my eyes and trust that
my Father is walking with me."*

# Walk By Faith

*"Today, I've decided to close my eyes and trust that
my Father is walking with me."*

# Walk By Faith

*"Today, I've decided to close my eyes and trust that
my Father is walking with me."*

# Walk By Faith

*"Today, I've decided to close my eyes and trust that
my Father is walking with me."*

# Walk By Faith

_____

_____

_____

_____

_____

_____

_____

_____

_____

_____

_____

_____

_____

_____

_____

_____

_____

_____

_____

_____

*"Today, I've decided to close my eyes and trust that
my Father is walking with me."*

# Walk By Faith

# Walk By Faith

*"Today, I've decided to close my eyes and trust that my Father is walking with me."*

# Walk By Faith

_"Today, I've decided to close my eyes and trust that_
_my Father is walking with me."_

# Walk By Faith

_"Today, I've decided to close my eyes and trust that
my Father is walking with me."_

# Walk By Faith

*"Today, I've decided to close my eyes and trust that my Father is walking with me."*

# Walk By Faith

_"Today, I've decided to close my eyes and trust that
my Father is walking with me."_

# Walk By Faith

_____
_____
_____
_____
_____
_____
_____
_____
_____
_____
_____
_____
_____
_____
_____
_____
_____
_____
_____
_____

*"Today, I've decided to close my eyes and trust that
my Father is walking with me."*

# Walk By Faith

*"Today, I've decided to close my eyes and trust that
my Father is walking with me."*

# Walk By Faith

*"Today, I've decided to close my eyes and trust that
my Father is walking with me."*

# Walk By Faith

_"Today, I've decided to close my eyes and trust that my Father is walking with me."_

# Walk By Faith

_"Today, I've decided to close my eyes and trust that_
_my Father is walking with me."_

# Walk By Faith

_____

_____

_____

_____

_____

_____

_____

_____

_____

_____

_____

_____

_____

_____

_____

_____

_____

_____

*"Today, I've decided to close my eyes and trust that
my Father is walking with me."*

# Walk By Faith

_"Today, I've decided to close my eyes and trust that
my Father is walking with me."_

# Walk By Faith

*"Today, I've decided to close my eyes and trust that my Father is walking with me."*

# Walk By Faith

*"Today, I've decided to close my eyes and trust that my Father is walking with me."*

# Walk By Faith

*"Today, I've decided to close my eyes and trust that
my Father is walking with me."*

# Walk By Faith

_"Today, I've decided to close my eyes and trust that
my Father is walking with me."_

# Walk By Faith

*"Today, I've decided to close my eyes and trust that
my Father is walking with me."*

# Walk By Faith

_"Today, I've decided to close my eyes and trust that my Father is walking with me."_

# Walk By Faith

*"Today, I've decided to close my eyes and trust that my Father is walking with me."*

# Walk By Faith

*"Today, I've decided to close my eyes and trust that
my Father is walking with me."*

# Walk By Faith

*"Today, I've decided to close my eyes and trust that my Father is walking with me."*

# Walk By Faith

*"Today, I've decided to close my eyes and trust that my Father is walking with me."*

# Walk By Faith

_"Today, I've decided to close my eyes and trust that
my Father is walking with me."_

# Walk By Faith

*"Today, I've decided to close my eyes and trust that
my Father is walking with me."*

# Walk By Faith

*"Today, I've decided to close my eyes and trust that my Father is walking with me."*

# Walk By Faith

*"Today, I've decided to close my eyes and trust that
my Father is walking with me."*

# Walk By Faith

*"Today, I've decided to close my eyes and trust that my Father is walking with me."*

# Walk By Faith

*"Today, I've decided to close my eyes and trust that
my Father is walking with me."*

# Walk By Faith

*"Today, I've decided to close my eyes and trust that
my Father is walking with me."*

# Walk By Faith

_"Today, I've decided to close my eyes and trust that my Father is walking with me."_

# Walk By Faith

*"Today, I've decided to close my eyes and trust that my Father is walking with me."*

# Walk By Faith

*"Today, I've decided to close my eyes and trust that my Father is walking with me."*

# Walk By Faith

*"Today, I've decided to close my eyes and trust that
my Father is walking with me."*

# Walk By Faith

*"Today, I've decided to close my eyes and trust that
my Father is walking with me."*

# Walk By Faith

*"Today, I've decided to close my eyes and trust that my Father is walking with me."*

# Walk By Faith

*"Today, I've decided to close my eyes and trust that
my Father is walking with me."*

# Walk By Faith

# Walk By Faith

*"Today, I've decided to close my eyes and trust that my Father is walking with me."*

# Walk By Faith

*"Today, I've decided to close my eyes and trust that my Father is walking with me."*

# Walk By Faith

*"Today, I've decided to close my eyes and trust that my Father is walking with me."*

# Walk By Faith

*"Today, I've decided to close my eyes and trust that
my Father is walking with me."*

# Walk By Faith

_"Today, I've decided to close my eyes and trust that
my Father is walking with me."_

# Walk By Faith

_"Today, I've decided to close my eyes and trust that my Father is walking with me."_

# Walk By Faith

*"Today, I've decided to close my eyes and trust that
my Father is walking with me."*

# Walk By Faith

*"Today, I've decided to close my eyes and trust that
my Father is walking with me."*

# Walk By Faith

*"Today, I've decided to close my eyes and trust that my Father is walking with me."*

# Walk By Faith

_____
_____
_____
_____
_____
_____
_____
_____
_____
_____
_____
_____
_____
_____
_____
_____
_____
_____
_____

*"Today, I've decided to close my eyes and trust that
my Father is walking with me."*

# Walk By Faith

*"Today, I've decided to close my eyes and trust that my Father is walking with me."*

# Walk By Faith

_"Today, I've decided to close my eyes and trust that
my Father is walking with me."_

# Walk By Faith

*"Today, I've decided to close my eyes and trust that my Father is walking with me."*

# Walk By Faith

_"Today, I've decided to close my eyes and trust that
my Father is walking with me."_

# Walk By Faith

*"Today, I've decided to close my eyes and trust that my Father is walking with me."*

# Walk By Faith

*"Today, I've decided to close my eyes and trust that
my Father is walking with me."*

www.ingramcontent.com/pod-product-compliance
Lightning Source LLC
Chambersburg PA
CBHW030514100426
42813CB00001B/38